93-652

J
591.092   Fromer, Julie
Fro   Jane Goodall, living
        with the chimps

JANE GOODALL

Living with the Chimps

Earth Keepers

JANE GOODALL

Living with the Chimps

Julie Fromer
Illustrated by Antonio Castro

Twenty-First Century Books

A Division of Henry Holt and Co., Inc.

Frederick, Maryland

Published by
Twenty-First Century Books
A Division of Henry Holt and Co., Inc.
38 South Market Street
Frederick, Maryland 21701

Text Copyright © 1992
Twenty-First Century Books

Illustrations Copyright © 1992
Twenty-First Century Books

Printed in Mexico

10 9 8 7 6 5 4 3 2 1

Library of Congress Cataloging in Publication Data

Fromer, Julie
Jane Goodall: Living with the Chimps
Illustrated by Antonio Castro

(An Earth Keepers Book)
Includes glossary and index.
Summary: A biography of the woman whose methods of studying
chimpanzees became a model for wildlife observation.
1. Goodall, Jane, 1934- —Juvenile literature.
2. Chimpanzees—Tanzania—Gombe Stream National Park—Juvenile literature.
3. Primatologists—England—Biography—Juvenile literature.
4. Gombe Stream National Park (Tanzania)—Juvenile literature.
[1. Goodall, Jane, 1934- . 2. Zoologists. 3. Chimpanzees.]
I. Castro, Antonio, 1941- , ill. II. Title.
III. Series: Earth Keepers
QL31.G58F76   1992
591'.092—dc20 [B] 91-41057 CIP AC
ISBN 0-8050-2116-7

CONTENTS

"Chimpanzees have given me so much."

Chapter 1

Part of Their World

The slender woman with a graying ponytail was out of breath. She had followed a group of chimps as they climbed up one of the steep ridges of the Gombe National Park. The chimps feasted on the fruit of nearby trees, and Jane Goodall settled back to survey the African landscape.

A great deal had changed since Jane Goodall first saw the forested valleys of East Africa. When she arrived in Africa more than 30 years earlier, the forest stretched far into the distance, across rugged valleys as far as she could see. Ten thousand chimps made the forest their home.

Today, she knows, the forest home of the chimps—and the chimps themselves—are in danger of being wiped out.

Jane Goodall knows the world of the chimps better than anyone else. In 1960, at the age of 26, she entered the jungle to observe wild chimps in their natural habitat. She was the first person to attempt such a study, and her research became a model for wildlife observation.

To understand the chimps, Jane Goodall became a part of their world. For more than 30 years, she has lived with the wild chimps of Africa. Sharing their jungle habitat, she has observed the chimps closely and carefully—and recorded every detail of their lives.

She delighted in their playfulness. She was startled by their ability to learn. She was moved by the close bonds of friendship and family that the chimps formed. And she grieved with them over the death of a loved one.

What Goodall discovered by living with the chimps took many scientists by surprise. She learned that chimps are highly intelligent animals. They can think and make plans. They are very social by nature, forming close and lasting relationships. They are capable of feeling and expressing a range of emotions—joy and sadness, pleasure and fear, anger and love.

Before Goodall went to Africa, most people thought that only human beings possessed these traits. What she learned has changed not only the way we think about animals, but the way we think about ourselves—and our place in nature—as well.

Jane Goodall continues to study the wild chimpanzee. Grateful for what the chimps of Africa have given to her, she believes that it is now time to help them. Today, she

works to conserve the habitats of the wild chimps and to promote better treatment for chimps held in captivity.

"Chimpanzees have given me so much in my life," she says. "The least I can do is to speak out for those who cannot speak for themselves."

Chapter 2

A Good Noticer

Jane Goodall was born in London, England, on April 3, 1934. Her father, Mortimer, was a businessman, and her mother, Myfanwe (known to everyone as Vanne), took care of their home.

Jane's earliest memories reveal her interest in living things. Even in the midst of such a busy city, she enjoyed the world of nature. As an infant, Jane was often taken in her baby carriage to the many parks in London. The London Zoo was also a favorite place to visit.

Once, a man standing by Jane's carriage caught and crushed a large, colorful dragonfly that had been hovering over her. "I cried and cried," she recalls, "not because I was afraid, but because I felt bad that such a pretty thing was destroyed."

When Jane was a little over a year old, her mother gave her a toy chimpanzee. It was "a large, hairy model celebrating the birth of the first chimpanzee infant ever born in the London Zoo," Jane remembers. "Most of my mother's friends were horrified. They predicted that the ghastly creature would give a small child nightmares." But Jane loved the stuffed toy. Jubilee (named for the infant chimpanzee in the zoo) was dark and furry, with pale, stitched hands and feet. He was just about the same size as Jane.

When Jane was four years old, her sister, Judy, was born. The next year, 1939, the Goodalls moved to Bournemouth, a resort town on the southern coast of England. Jane and her family moved into a big, brick house on the edge of the town. The rocky cliffs that towered above the English Channel were just a few blocks away.

Jane's parents divorced when she was eight years old, and her father returned to London to pursue his business career. Jane Goodall doesn't speak much about her father, and little is known about her relationship with him. But after the divorce, Jane grew even closer to her mother. Vanne was pleased that her elder daughter showed an interest in nature. She wanted to nourish within Jane a sense of wonder about living things, a feeling of adventure and excitement in discovering the natural world.

At Bournemouth, Jane found that live animals were even more fascinating than toy ones. With the English Channel only a short walk away, Jane spent much of her time outside, looking at the animals near her new home. She watched sea gulls swoop over the waves. She played in the tidepools that formed along the pebbly shore.

Jane attended a private school near Bournemouth, but she always preferred the kinds of lessons that were taught by nature. "Although I always did well in my studies, I never liked school," she remarked. "I just wanted to be outdoors, watching and learning."

Watching and learning about nature, Jane discovered, is not always easy. Animals may not cooperate with the people who are trying to study them. But even at an early age, Jane found creative ways to observe the local wildlife. Puzzled by the fact that, each day, eggs seemed to appear magically in a hen house not far from home, Jane decided to see for herself how the process occurred.

One morning, Jane Goodall wriggled her way through the narrow opening of the chicken house. She remained hidden inside the cramped, stuffy shed for more than five hours, sitting calmly in the straw beside the hens. "The whole household had apparently been searching for me for hours, and my mother had even rung the police to report me missing," she wrote.

However, when Jane finally came out of the hen house, her hair tangled with straw, she was not punished. Vanne understood her daughter's curiosity. "She recognized my patience with animals and encouraged me to study them," Jane said.

As Jane read stories about animals, her love of nature grew. At the age of seven, she read *The Story of Doctor Dolittle*, by Hugh Lofting. At once, Jane was entranced by the imaginary adventures of this odd Englishman who could talk to animals.

The friendly doctor, who traveled all over the world, had developed a rather unusual method for choosing a destination. He would close his eyes and open a large atlas of the world. Without looking at the page, Doctor Dolittle would then take a pencil and stick it down on the opened book. And wherever the pencil landed was the next place he would go.

In these stories, Jane read about little Tommy Stubbins, who became great friends with the doctor. She understood how Tommy felt as he sat by the river that ran through the imaginary town of Puddleby. Tommy described how he dreamed of sailing off to lands that he had never seen:

> *"I used to go down and watch the sailors unloading the ships upon the river-wall. The sailors sang strange songs as they pulled upon the ropes; and I learned these songs by heart. And I would sit on the river-wall with my feet dangling over the water and sing with the men, pretending to myself that I too was a sailor."*

After she read Dolittle's descriptions of Africa, Jane Goodall was sure that she wanted to go there, too. "That's when I first decided that someday I had to go to Africa," she said. Like Tommy Stubbins, she "longed always to sail away with those brave ships . . . to go with them out into the world to seek my fortune in foreign lands."

Reading about the doctor's talking parrot, Polynesia, taught Jane an important lesson about nature. "Are you a good noticer?" Polynesia asked Tommy Stubbins. "Do you notice things well?" Polynesia explained that "being a good noticer is terribly important" in learning the facts about animals:

> *"That is what you call powers of observation— noticing the small things about birds and animals: the way they walk and move their heads and flip their wings; the way they sniff the air and twitch their whiskers and wiggle their tails. You have to notice all those little things."*

Jane was so interested in "noticing" animals that she started her own wildlife journal in which she kept detailed records of her observations. She found out, for instance, which clumps of grass concealed the entrances to rabbit burrows. Hidden in the tall grass nearby, she would wait quietly until twilight, when the gray-brown rabbits would come out to nibble fresh shoots of clover. Then, Jane would carefully write down how many animals she saw and how far they hopped that evening.

As Jane grew older, she read as much as she could about animal behavior, and her journal grew larger and more detailed. She continued to dream of Africa. The more she read about Africa and the creatures living there, the more she hoped to study the wildlife of that vast continent.

Jane moved to London when she was 18 and enrolled in a secretarial program. "Mum said secretaries could get jobs anywhere in the world," she remarked, "and I still felt my destiny lay in Africa."

Jane worked for a while as a secretary. But when a friend from school invited Jane to visit her family's farm in Kenya, an East African country, she was more than ready to accept. The chance that Jane Goodall was waiting for had finally arrived.

Chapter 3

African Journey

In 1957, a young woman, slender and delicate looking, stepped down from the ship that had brought her to the port of Mombasa, on the coast of Kenya. Her ash-blond hair was pulled out of the way into a long ponytail. Now 23 years old, Jane Goodall was at last in the land she had dreamed about.

Africa is the second largest continent (only Asia is bigger), occupying one-fifth of the total land surface of the world. It is three times larger than the United States. A land of great variety, Africa is home to more than 3,000 ethnic groups who speak 1,000 different languages. The African landscape ranges from the immense sand dunes of the Sahara Desert (the largest desert in the world) to the dense rain forests of central Africa. Huge herds of wild animals roam the countryside only a few miles from the glass-and-steel buildings of modern cities.

Much of Africa is covered by vast, dry grasslands, or savannahs. These savannahs are found on the high plateau that forms the interior of the continent. To the east, the great plateau begins to rise, creating the cliffs and mountains of East Africa. There, trade winds from the Indian Ocean bring heavy, mid-day thunderstorms to drench the African jungle.

From Mombasa, Goodall traveled to her friend's farm, where she enjoyed a pleasant vacation. However, instead of returning to England, she decided to stay in Africa. Goodall moved to Nairobi, the capital of Kenya, and took what she described as a "dreary office job."

"If you are interested in animals," Goodall was told, "then you should meet Dr. Leakey." Dr. Louis Leakey was the head of the Coryndon Museum (now called the National Museum of Natural History) in Nairobi. Leakey and his wife, Mary, were anthropologists. They studied ancient life through the fossil remains of creatures that lived millions of years ago. At Olduvai Gorge and other sites in East Africa, the Leakeys searched for traces of the earliest ancestors of human beings, called hominids.

Soon after her arrival in Nairobi, Jane Goodall paid a visit to Dr. Leakey. "He must have sensed that my interest in animals was not just a passing phase, but was rooted deep," Goodall said, "because on the spot he gave me a job as an assistant secretary."

Goodall worked at the museum in Nairobi until the Leakeys asked her to join one of their trips to Olduvai Gorge on the plains of the Serengeti National Park. The Serengeti is located south of Kenya, in northern Tanzania. (In 1958, when Goodall was working for the Leakeys, the country was still known by its original name, Tanganyika, a Swahili word that means "widespread forestland." After Tanganyika gained its independence from Great Britain, it united with the tiny island nation of Zanzibar. The two countries joined their names to produce "Tanzania.")

In a continent as diverse as Africa, Tanzania contains some of the greatest differences of all. The coastal plain is a hot and humid region. The dry, central plateau is broken by the Great Rift Valley, a 3,000-mile-long fault in the earth's crust. Snowcapped mountains rise above endless grasslands, clear lakes, and dense forests.

Mount Kilimanjaro, the highest peak in Africa, is just south of the Kenyan border, not far from the Serengeti. The lowest elevation in Africa is also found in Tanzania. At the bottom of Lake Tanganyika, which forms part of the Great Rift Valley, the elevation sinks to 2,000 feet below sea level.

The largest herds of wild animals in the world roam the 6,000 square miles of the Serengeti National Park. More than a million animals inhabit this area. Enormous groups of antelopes cross the plains in their search for food and water. Zebras and wildebeests, watchful for signs of lions or other predators, graze on the vast grasslands. In the shadow of Mount Kilimanjaro, giraffes reach for their evening meal. The park is home to the elephant, rhinoceros, waterbuck, baboon, and more than 200 types of birds.

Just outside the southwestern boundary of the park is Olduvai Gorge. Part of the Great Rift Valley, it is a 25-mile-long ravine. Millions of years ago, Olduvai was the site of a large lake where animals came in search of water and where early humans made their homes.

Goodall worked each day in the heat of the African sun, digging for fossils in Olduvai Gorge. Large shovels might damage the delicate fossil remains, so the diggers had to use small hand trowels and dental picks to scrape away the ancient African soil. "It was fascinating work," Goodall remembers:

> *"For hours, as I picked away at the ancient clay or rock of the Olduvai to extract the remains of creatures that had lived millions of years ago, the task would be purely routine. But from time to time, without warning, I would be filled with awe by the sight or the feel of some bone I held in my hand. This—this very bone— had once been part of a living, breathing animal."*

Carefully inspecting the bone of some ancient animal, Jane Goodall tried to picture what this "living, breathing animal" had really been like. "What had it looked like?" she wondered. "What color was its hair? What was the odor of its body?"

When their work was finished, Goodall and another assistant would climb back up to their camp on the dry plains above the gorge. As the Serengeti plains cooled each evening, the animals that had rested during the heat of the day slowly emerged.

"We walked past the low thorn bushes," Jane Goodall wrote, "and often glimpsed dik-diks, graceful miniature antelopes scarcely larger than a hare. Sometimes, there would be a small herd of gazelles or giraffes, and on a few memorable occasions we saw a black rhinoceros plodding along the gorge below."

Goodall loved to observe the creatures of the Serengeti, so different from the animals of her home. Once, she came face to face with a young male lion. Goodall slowly backed away as the lion curiously observed her.

Although the work with fossils intrigued her, Goodall felt drawn to the animals that inhabited the plains. "I still wanted to study living creatures," she recalls. "I wanted to come as close to talking to the animals as I could—to be like Doctor Dolittle."

Louis Leakey understood Goodall's dream of studying wildlife. He wanted to know more about the creatures whose ancient bones he was uncovering. He wondered how they behaved. He was curious about their families and social groups.

Leakey had an idea that might help him to find the answers to some of these questions—and give his assistant a chance to study the wild animals of Africa. He thought that a long-term study of chimpanzees in their natural habitat would help scientists understand the behavior of early human beings.

If humans had descended from an apelike ancestor, Leakey explained, then "an understanding of chimpanzee behavior today might shed light on the behavior of our stone-age ancestors." As Goodall later said, Leakey hoped that the wild chimps "would provide a new window onto our own past."

This kind of a study had never been attempted before. Chimps had been studied only in captivity, in laboratories or in zoos. But as both Leakey and Goodall knew, animals kept in captivity do not behave the way they do in the wild. Caged in pens, chimpanzees may become sullen and withdrawn, or bad-tempered and vicious.

Leakey suggested to Goodall that a good place for a scientific study of wild chimpanzees would be the Gombe Stream Chimpanzee Reserve (now the Gombe National Park), a protected area located in western Tanzania, along the shore of Lake Tanganyika. He described the reserve as a rugged, mountainous, and isolated area.

"It was completely cut off from civilization," Goodall wrote. Leakey spoke of the dedication and patience that would be required of any person who tried to study chimpanzees in the wild. Such a study might take as long as 10 years, he warned.

Goodall was surprised that Leakey asked her to be responsible for such an important study. "Although it was the sort of thing I most wanted to do, I was not qualified to undertake a scientific study of animal behavior," she admitted. But Leakey said that he did not believe that Jane Goodall needed a university training. He felt that she would bring to this study two things more valuable than a university degree: a desire for knowledge and an understanding of animals.

Jane Goodall had her own reason for going to Gombe. She knew that the wild chimps of Africa were in danger. Their forest habitat was being rapidly destroyed for what Goodall called "the ever-growing needs of ever-growing human populations."

Each year, farms, roads, and houses cut deeper and deeper into the jungle homes of the chimpanzees. Logging and mining operations were taking away more and more of the forest. Human diseases were killing many animals.

And human beings were killing many more—hunting them for food, or killing females so that their infants might be sold as pets or laboratory animals.

"The aim of my field study was to discover as much as possible about the way of life of the chimpanzee," Jane Goodall wrote, "before it was too late."

Chapter 4

The Proudest Moment

Jane Goodall returned to England, where she learned everything she could about chimpanzees. She discovered that the chimp is the closest animal relative to human beings. No other animal resembles human beings more than the wild chimpanzee.

Part of the ape family (which also includes the gorilla, the orangutan, and the gibbon), chimpanzees live in the dense forests of central and western Africa. They live in groups that range in size from 10 to 80 animals. Each chimp group inhabits a jungle territory that covers about 10 square miles.

Adult male chimps may grow to be up to five feet tall (when standing upright) and weigh about 120 pounds. Females are a bit smaller. In the wild, chimps live to be between 30 and 40 years old. They spend most of their day gathering their favorite foods, such as fruit and leaves.

By June 1960, Jane Goodall was back in Nairobi. She was ready to begin the journey to Kigoma, the nearest town to the Gombe reserve. But the government officials in Kigoma "would not hear of a young girl living in the bush alone without a companion," Goodall wrote. So her mother, Vanne, agreed to accompany Jane into the forests of Africa.

Goodall and her mother drove to Kigoma in a rickety car overloaded with their supplies. Bumping along the rough, dirt roads for three days, they passed through the swaying grasses of the broad savannah. At night, Jane and Vanne set up their camp on the dark plains, huddled together by the fire they built to warn away any curious (and unfriendly) animals.

As they drove west, the land rose, becoming hillier and cooler. Finally, they reached Kigoma, on the shore of Lake Tanganyika. Mango trees threw their welcome shade along the town's main street. "The hub of activity was down by the lake shore," Goodall observed, "where the natural harbor offers anchorage to the boats plying up and down the lake."

The fruit and vegetable markets of Kigoma displayed a colorful array of bananas, oranges, and the dark purple passion fruit. The *dukas*, or town stores, stocked almost anything Goodall might need. One store owner showed her how to wear the squares of brightly colored material called *kangas*: one square, wrapped around under the arms, hangs down just below the knees; the other square is used to make a fashionable native headdress.

After a week in Kigoma, the game ranger for the area took Jane and Vanne in a small boat along the shore of the lake to the reserve. The deep lake was remarkably clear. The boat chugged slowly northward. To the east, Goodall saw a series of low, densely forested valleys.

Steep mountains rose from the strip of beach, separating the valleys with high, wooded ridges and rocky peaks. Little fishing boats skimmed the water along the shore, and villages of mud-and-grass huts dotted the lower slopes of the mountains.

Goodall looked at the forests where she would spend so much time. She could not help but be nervous about the future. "How easily would I be able to find my way around the rugged country?" she wondered. "How long would it take the chimpanzees to get used to me? Would it be easy to find them?"

"But more than any other feeling," she later wrote, "excitement welled up within me as I tried to guess what lay ahead."

After two hours, the boat landed at Kasakela, about halfway up the 10-mile shore of the Gombe reserve. A crowd of curious villagers met Goodall and her mother on the beach.

With "great ceremony," Jane Goodall remembers, they were introduced to Iddi Matata, the honorary headman of the village. Matata welcomed them in Swahili, his native language, so Goodall understood little of his long speech. It would take many years for her to learn the soft, flowing language of her adopted homeland.

Goodall and her mother set up their camp in a small clearing in the woods. Once things were in order, Goodall decided to investigate her new home. The sun was shining fiercely; the air was dry and hot. Jane Goodall climbed the slippery cliff behind the camp. She reached a big, flat rock that offered a good view of the valley around her.

A troop of about 60 baboons wandered by, looking for insects and seeds in an area cleared by a recent brush fire. The baboons displayed some signs of alarm, shaking branches and barking, when they discovered this strange creature perched on the rock. But they soon lost interest in the newcomer and continued on their way.

The forest hummed and chirped around her. She took a deep breath, inhaling the dark, rich smell of the soil and the fresh, green fragrance of the trees. The rock beneath her felt warm and alive from the setting sun, which flickered orange and red through the forest leaves. Goodall no longer felt like a stranger in the jungle. "I knew then that my dream had come true," she said.

In the evening darkness, she felt at peace with her surroundings and herself. "I was well aware of the many difficulties facing me," she wrote. "But I knew the day was one of the happiest of my life. That night, after supper around a campfire, I pulled my low bed out beneath the palm trees and slept under the stars."

For months, Goodall searched the forest for the wild chimpanzees. She often heard their noisy "pant-hoots"— loud hooting calls punctuated by inhaled breaths. "The sound was thrilling beyond words," she wrote. She also heard the echoing sound of excited chimps drumming on tree trunks, rapidly beating on the wood with their feet. Through her binoculars, Jane Goodall could see groups of chimpanzees feeding in the trees, but she could never get close enough to observe individual animals. Whenever she tried to approach closer than 500 yards, the shy chimps fled into the forest.

Jane Goodall was disappointed that she could barely see the animals she was supposed to be studying. But those first weeks at the Gombe reserve helped her adjust to the rugged African landscape.

"My skin became hardened to the rough grasses of the valleys," Goodall recalls, "and I became increasingly sure-footed on the treacherous slopes." The African guides who at first accompanied Goodall into the jungle taught her much about the land and its inhabitants, both animal and human.

Goodall's mother, Vanne, helped to win the good will of the African villagers. Vanne had begun giving out first-aid supplies and simple medicines to sick villagers. Soon, people traveled for miles to reach her makeshift clinic. Slowly, the African people lost their suspicion of these foreign women who wanted to trek through the dense forest looking for wildlife.

"How lucky I was to have a mother like Vanne—a mother in a million," Goodall remarked. "I could not have done without her during those early days."

Vanne was Jane's scientific assistant as well as her constant friend. "She helped me to keep up my spirits during the depressing weeks when I could get nowhere near the chimps," Goodall explained.

But after five months, Vanne had to return to England. Dr. Leakey sent his assistant Hassan to join Goodall. Hassan had been Leakey's helper for 15 years, and his warm, confident manner reassured Vanne as she left her daughter in the African forest.

"The trial period was over," Goodall said. She had adjusted to the solitary life of a wildlife observer. "The forest no longer seemed hostile after I learned to creep along pig trails instead of forcing my way through the undergrowth," she wrote. "The slopes were no longer a nightmare when I had discovered the baboon trails where I could pull myself up the steepest parts by roots worn smooth by constant use."

Though the chimps still refused to cooperate, Goodall was able to observe many other animals. There were the gray bush pigs, striped mongooses, and spotted elephant shrews. She often saw baboons from the troops that made the nearby area their home. Other monkeys lived in the valleys of Gombe, such as red colobus, redtail, blue, and silver monkeys.

"I never attempted to hide," Goodall wrote. Gradually, the animals became used to the human who had invaded their jungle territory. As the months passed, however, she worried that she had learned nothing about chimpanzees.

One day, Goodall set off for the mountain that she had climbed on her first day at Gombe. In her dull-colored shorts (the wild animals were alarmed by bright colors), she made her way up the steep and slippery slope. She reached the large, rocky peak that offered such a good view of the forested mountains.

Resting on the Peak, as the rocky outcropping came to be known, Goodall searched for chimpanzees through her binoculars. The gentle slopes of the mountains, looking smooth and green from her position, spread away from her for miles, rising to the craggy ridges that led to the neighboring valleys.

As she caught her breath on the Peak, Jane Goodall noticed two male chimpanzees less than 20 yards away. The chimps stared at her for a few minutes, but instead of scampering away, they moved calmly into the undergrowth. Later in the morning, Goodall saw other groups of chimps crossing the paths of the mountain below her. They were feeding on the fruit of the wild fig trees.

As each group of chimps passed by, they gave Goodall a surprised look, then hastened to join the noisy gathering in the fig trees. After feeding for a time, they climbed down and wandered away from the area.

"They walked up the valley," Goodall wrote. "I could see them following each other in a long, orderly line. Two small infants were perched like jockeys on their mothers' backs. I even saw them pause to drink, each one for about a minute, before leaping across the stream."

For over a year, Jane Goodall had been trying to overcome the chimps' fear of her. Now the chimps were so close that she could hear them breathing.

"Without any doubt," Goodall wrote, "this was the proudest moment I had known."

*"I accepted aloneness as a way of
life, and I was no longer lonely."*

Chapter 5

A Window on Nature

The fig season lasted for about eight weeks, giving Goodall the opportunity to watch the chimps every day from the Peak. Once the chimps discovered that there was nothing to fear from Goodall, they began to accept her as part of their jungle world. And, slowly, she began to learn about the chimps' way of life.

Within the larger chimp community, various smaller groups constantly formed and then changed as members traveled with other chimpanzees. Goodall witnessed the aggressive charging displays of the male chimps, when they rush down the jungle slopes, hooting and dragging branches, stamping the ground and beating on trees. She observed the social, gentle side of chimp behavior: long grooming sessions, when chimps clean one another's fur and delight in touching, patting, and embracing.

Goodall knew how important it was to be a "good noticer." She learned to read the facial expressions of the chimps and understand the meaning of their hoots and shouts. Days, weeks, and months of patient observations were carefully recorded:

"I saw youngsters having wild games through the treetops, chasing around after each other or jumping again and again, one after the other, from a branch to a springy bough below."

"During the heat of midday or after a long spell of feeding, I saw the adults grooming each other, carefully looking through the hair of their companions. I saw one female, newly arrived in a group, hurry up to a big male and hold her hand toward him. He reached out, clasped her hand in his, drew it toward him, and kissed it with his lips."

Jane Goodall watched the chimps from daybreak until dusk. She slept nearby so she would be there when they woke up in the morning. The chimpanzees made large, leafy nests, pulling branches together until the pile was soft and springy.

If the bed wasn't quite comfortable, the chimps would often pick up a handful of leaves to use as a pillow. On the jungle floor, Goodall wrapped herself up in a blanket and slept on the hard ground.

During these days, Jane Goodall was completely on her own, alone except for the chimpanzees. She enjoyed these quiet days in the African forest. "I accepted aloneness as a way of life," Goodall said, "and I was no longer lonely. I was utterly absorbed in the work, fascinated by the chimps."

The thick, hot forest was the chimps' home, and in order to understand their lives, Goodall had to make the forest her home, too. She wanted to become a part of the forest, like the chimps she had come so far to observe:

> *"I longed to be able to swing through the branches like the chimps, to sleep in the treetops lulled by the rustling of the leaves in the breeze. I loved to sit in a forest when it was raining, to hear the pattering of the drops on the leaves and feel utterly enclosed in a dim twilight world of greens and browns and dampness."*

Spending every day with the chimps, Jane Goodall began to recognize individuals. "As soon as I was sure of knowing a chimpanzee if I saw it again, I named it. Some scientists feel that animals should be labeled by numbers," Goodall remarked, "but I have always been interested in the differences between individuals. A name is not only more individual but also far easier to remember."

The first chimp that Goodall named was Mr. McGregor. He reminded Goodall of the gardener in *The Tale of Peter Rabbit*. Mr. McGregor was easy to recognize because the top of his head, his neck, and his shoulders were nearly hairless, which is unusual in chimpanzees. "With his bare crown and his fondness for walking upright, Mr. McGregor looks like a strange old man of the forest," Goodall said.

Olly was easy to spot, thanks to her long face and a thick fluff of hair on the back of her head. This old female chimp was accompanied by her young daughter and son. Goodall felt that William, an adult male, must have been Olly's brother. "I never saw any special signs of friendship between them," she said, "but their faces were amazingly alike. They both had long upper lips that wobbled when they turned their heads."

Goodall also knew by sight old Flo, with her big nose and ragged ears. "Flo really is ugly," Goodall reported. "Yet she has as much character as a whole platoon of the other chimps." With Flo was her family—her two-year-old daughter, Fifi, and her six-year-old son, Figan.

David Graybeard, an adult male chimp with a silvery-gray chin, helped to make the chimp community more comfortable with their human observer. He was always quite relaxed when Goodall met him in the forest. Then, one day, he showed up at the camp down the mountain. The chimps did not usually wander so far away from the safety of the forest.

"After all the months of despair, when the chimpanzees had fled at the sight of me," Goodall wrote, "here was one making himself at home in our very camp."

One of David's camp visits made a particularly strong impression on Goodall. She was sitting outside her tent when David climbed down from a tree and walked toward her. Goodall saw that his hair was standing on end, a sign that David was angry or frustrated. "All at once," Goodall wrote, "he ran straight at me, snatched a banana from my table, and hurried off to eat it further away."

Goodall began leaving out bananas at the camp feeding station for this new visitor. "Soon David began popping into camp any old day," she recalls, and he brought his friends along, too.

Goliath, a large, powerful male, and William began to show up regularly. Flo and her family came next, and gradually more chimps appeared, providing Jane Goodall with a unique opportunity to observe them.

Goodall's acceptance by the chimps soon led to some remarkable observations. One day, she saw a small gathering of chimps below the Peak. Goodall clambered down the mountain to see what was so interesting.

She saw a male chimp holding a "pink-looking object from which he was from time to time pulling pieces with his teeth." A female and a youngster were begging for some. When the female "picked up a piece of the pink thing and put it to her mouth," Goodall knew that she had made a startling discovery. "It was at this moment that I realized the chimps were eating meat," she said.

Scientists had believed that chimps were vegetarians, eating mainly fruits and leaves, and on occasion a tasty insect. But Jane Goodall's research proved that chimpanzees are omnivorous: they eat both meat and vegetables, as well as fruit, nuts, and seeds. Later, she also observed the chimps hunting, purposefully killing young bush pigs and monkeys for meat.

Two weeks after she had seen the chimps eating meat, Goodall reported that she saw something that excited her even more. The hot, dry days of summer had given way to the start of the rainy season. "The blackened slopes were softened by feathery new grass shoots," she noted, "and in some places the ground was carpeted by a variety of flowers."

All morning, she had tramped through the valleys, searching for the chimps but never hearing a hoot. Pulling herself up the slopes, she moved toward the Peak. Seeing a movement in the grass, she focused her binoculars. There was David Graybeard. He was "squatting beside the red earth mound of a termite nest." Goodall cautiously pushed through the long grass to see what he was doing. She recorded David's activity:

> "I saw him carefully push a long grass stem down into a hole in the mound. After a moment he withdrew it and picked something from the end with his mouth. I was too far away to make out what he was eating, but it was obvious that he was actually using a grass stem as a tool."

After a few minutes, the grass stem bent, and David Graybeard discarded it. He picked a length of vine, and "with a sweeping movement of one hand, he stripped the leaves from the vine, bit a piece from one end, and set to work again with his prepared tool." Fishing for termites, David Graybeard had not only used a tool to reach the termites, he had also made a tool, changing the vine so that it worked even better.

Before Jane Goodall went to Africa, it was commonly believed that humans were the only animals that made tools. But Goodall observed that chimps, too, make and use tools, creating new ones when new situations arise. She also discovered that this tool-making activity, like so much that the wild chimps do, is learned behavior, an activity or tradition passed down from one generation to the next.

Louis Leakey had been right about Jane Goodall. Her desire to understand the chimps—to understand them as they really are in the wild—led her to endure the harsh and lonely life of the jungle. Her love for the chimps was rewarded with a series of discoveries that enlarged our view of animal behavior. And her patience and dedication opened a new window on the world of nature—a window that no one had ever looked through before.

Chapter 6

The Ways of the Forest

When Jane Goodall first came to Gombe, no one had spent more than a few months observing chimpanzees in the wild. Louis Leakey had told her that a thorough study of the chimps might take as long as 10 years. Privately, she thought that two or three years in the jungle would be long enough.

She was wrong about that.

Jane Goodall has now spent more than 30 years among the wild chimps of Gombe. The length of her study has enabled her to observe these animals over the course of several generations. Goodall has followed the cycles of birth and death in the Gombe chimp community. She has seen a new generation of chimps learn the ways of the forest, and she has watched many old friends pass away.

These years brought many changes to Goodall's life as well. In 1964, she married Hugo van Lawick, a wildlife photographer sent to Africa by the National Geographic

Society to film her work. Jane and Hugo made a quick return from their honeymoon when they received a letter from the camp at Gombe. "Flo amekwisha kuzaa," the Swahili message said. "Flo has had her baby."

Goodall was delighted when Flo brought the child to camp. "Cuddling her baby between belly and thigh, she came toward us on three limbs, followed by little Fifi and jaunty Figan," Goodall remembers. When the baby moved its head, Goodall could see "the pale-skinned face, the dark brilliant eyes, and the funny little one-sided mouth."

This was the first time that anyone had seen a chimpanzee infant in the wild. "We were filled with amazement that a wild chimpanzee mother trusted us enough to bring her baby close to us," Goodall said.

Goodall continued to watch the growth of Flint, Flo's infant. "As the months passed," Goodall reported, "we watched Flint change from a helpless baby to a small chimpanzee with a personality of his own." By doing so, she compiled the most detailed record of chimp development in the wild.

Like a human infant, a baby chimp is almost completely helpless. Using the strong muscles in its hands and feet, the chimp infant clings to its mother as she makes her daily round of the forest. As they get older, chimps start to move away from their mothers for short periods of time, but they run back at the least sign of danger.

Fifi was fascinated by her little brother. She would try to pull young Flint into her own embrace, but a protective Flo stopped her daughter from touching the infant. However, Goodall observed that as Flint got older, Flo allowed Fifi to cuddle and comfort her brother. In this way, Fifi learned how to be a chimp mother.

Another female chimp, Melissa, gave birth not long after Flo, and for the first time, Goodall saw a newborn chimpanzee, not even a day old. The baby's head lolled on its mother's knees. "Never had we imagined such a funny, twisted-up little face," Goodall recalls. She named the infant Goblin.

In 1967, Goodall's own son, Grub (his real name was Hugo), was born. To Jane, the camp at Gombe was a wonderful place for bringing up a child. Grub spent his early childhood "pottering about" the shores of Lake Tanganyika, swimming in the lake and making friends with the chimps who came to camp.

Jane claimed that she learned from the female chimps how important it is to establish "a close, affectionate bond" between mother and child. "I was determined to give my own child the best start I could," she said.

Jane set aside the afternoons as a special time to do things with Grub. But even in the jungle, a young boy has to go to school. When he was five, Grub began to take lessons from private tutors. At age nine, he was sent to a boarding school.

In 1974, Jane and Hugo were divorced. Later that year, Goodall married Derek Bryceson, who was the director of Tanzania's national parks. Bryceson died of cancer in 1980. Deep in grief over the death of her second husband, Goodall sought comfort among the chimps.

It was during this time, she reported, that she came closer to the chimps than ever before. "For I was with them not to observe," she wrote, "but simply because I needed their company."

The death of one of the chimps was always painful for Goodall. She went to Gombe simply to observe and record. But it was difficult for her not to feel a bond with the animals she had lived with for so many years.

61

When Flint was eight years old, his mother, Flo, died. Although Goodall knew that old Flo would have to die sometime, she was still saddened at the end. "I had known her for 11 years, and I had loved her," Goodall wrote. "I knew a real sense of loss, and I mourned as I have grieved at the passing of close human friends."

Goodall was surprised to see that this sense of loss, so familiar to humans, was shared by the chimps themselves. After his mother's death, Flint became depressed, and he would not leave her body. Fifi tried to encourage her brother to join the troop, but he would not move. Three weeks later, Flint was found dead—"very close," as Goodall noted, "to the spot where his mother had died."

It was David Graybeard's death that was the hardest for Jane Goodall to accept. "I felt a sorrow deeper than that which I have felt for any chimpanzee, before or since," Goodall said. It was David who had brought the chimps to Jane. "David Graybeard, gentle yet determined, calm and unafraid," she wrote, "opened my first window onto the chimpanzee's world."

"The chimpanzees got on with their lives," Goodall wrote. And she got on with hers. Goodall established a research center at Gombe, where students from around the world could continue her work. Their help allowed

Goodall to complete her education at Cambridge University and to record the behavior of the chimps in numerous articles and books.

Her first book, *In the Shadow of Man*, was published in 1971. "She is fascinated by her animals and describes with loving care each facet of their lives from birth to death," one reviewer said. Over the next 20 years, six more books and a series of television shows brought a vivid record of the chimps to millions of people.

Jane Goodall's work also brought to popular attention the dangers that the chimps face. As more and more of the forest is destroyed, as more and more animals are killed or captured, the number of wild chimps declines. The shadow of extinction hangs over their world.

Over the course of the last 30 years, the threat of extinction has increased. When Goodall arrived in Tanzania in 1960, there were as many as 10,000 chimps living there. By 1990, that number had declined to about 2,500. "Unless we act soon, our closest relatives may soon exist only in captivity," Goodall says.

Jane Goodall's fight to save the wild chimps is really a fight to preserve the order of the natural world. Her plea for the chimps is really a plea for human beings to learn that they, too, are part of that world.

For Jane Goodall, the permanent loss of the chimps would be a tragedy for human beings, too:

> *"The chimpanzee is only one of the many species threatened with extinction in the wild; but he is, after all, our closest living relative, and it would be tragic if, when our grandchildren are grown, the chimpanzee exists only in the zoo and the laboratory—a frightening thought, since for the most part the chimpanzee in captivity is very different from the magnificent creature we know so well in the wild."*

Goodall believes that when human beings endanger the order of nature, they also endanger themselves. If we continue to destroy the natural environment, Jane Goodall warns, "we shall, ourselves, be doomed."

*"Who knows what the next
decade will reveal?"*

Chapter 7

A Plea for the Chimps

Jane Goodall will never forget the first time she saw an adult male chimp being kept in a laboratory cage. His name was JoJo. He was housed in a medical laboratory in Sterling Forest, New York.

"I thought then of the chimpanzees of Gombe, free to roam the forests, free to play and groom and make nests in the springy branches," she recalls. "JoJo reached out a gentle finger and touched my cheek where the tears slid down my laboratory mask."

Since the 1980s, Goodall has been actively involved in efforts to protect the forest habitat of the chimps. The situation in Africa, she says, is grim. There is a desperate need for wildlife sanctuaries, protected areas where the endangered chimps can live in safety. In 1987, she founded the Jane Goodall Institute to serve as a center for wildlife research and conservation.

Goodall is equally troubled about the chimps who are held in captivity. "For years I was selfishly concerned only with the Gombe chimps," she admits. Now, Goodall says, she is worried about "the treatment and survival of chimps everywhere—in labs, in zoos, and in places where they're kept as pets or as amusements for tourists."

Of special concern to Goodall is the use of chimps for medical testing. "The chimpanzee is more like us than any other animal," she writes. "Are we justified in using an animal so close to us—an animal, moreover, that is highly endangered in its African forest home—as a human substitute in medical experiments?"

It is precisely because they are so closely related to humans that chimps are used in laboratory experiments. New medicines and medical procedures, considered too risky to use on humans, are routinely tested on chimps. Many scientists argue that such research plays an essential part in the battle against human disease.

According to Jane Goodall, the journey that the chimps endure from the forest to the laboratory is a painful and terrifying one. "The whole sickening business of capturing infant chimpanzees, for any purpose whatsoever, is not only cruel but also horribly wasteful," Goodall observes. Mothers attempt to protect their infants, and often both are killed. If other chimps try to interfere with a capture, they also are killed.

Once an infant is captured, the animal "is crammed into a tiny box or basket or pushed into a suffocating sack," Goodall reports. Many infants die during the trip, creating the demand for more chimps to be stolen from their mothers. Goodall estimates that "between 10 and 20 chimpanzees will die for every infant that survives."

The fate that awaits the chimps who survive capture, Goodall protests, "is so grim and wretched that it would have been better for them had they died during those bitter months when first they fell into human hands." The typical medical laboratory is lined with bare cages stacked one above the other. Inside these tiny cages, young chimps circle round and round or sit huddled in a deep sadness.

"Imagine being shut up in such a cell, with bars all around; bars on every side, bars above, bars below," Jane Goodall wrote in her most recent book, *Through a Window.* "With nothing to do. Nothing to wile away the monotony of the long, long days. No physical contact, ever, with another of your kind."

If animal testing is necessary, as many scientists claim, then better treatment of laboratory animals is necessary, too, Goodall insists. "We take from them their freedom, their health, and often their lives. Surely, the least we can do is try to provide them with some of the things that could make their imprisonment more bearable."

"The chimpanzees need our help now more than ever before," Goodall says. But she knows that this is not her fight alone:

> "We can only help if we each do our bit, no matter how small it may seem. If we don't, we are betraying not only the chimpanzees but also our own humanity. And we must never forget that, insurmountable as the environmental problems facing the world may seem, if we all pull together we have a good chance of bringing about change. We must. It is as simple as that!"

It has been more than 30 years since Goodall entered the African jungle. Today, she continues to study the wild chimps of Gombe. In fact, Jane Goodall is looking forward to a fourth decade of research. For her, there is always the excitement of discovery.

She hopes to learn even more about the wild animals she has come to know so well. "We have not been studying them for long enough," Goodall says. "Who knows what the next decade will reveal?"

Glossary

anthropology   the scientific study of the origin and behavior of human beings

ape   an animal belonging to the group that includes the chimpanzee, the gorilla, the orangutan, and the gibbon

captivity   when a wild animal is forcibly restrained or confined

charging display   loud and aggressive behavior used by male chimps to show dominance

conservation   the process by which natural resources are saved, or conserved

dukas   town stores

endangered species   a species that has so few members that it is in danger of becoming extinct

environment   the physical world that surrounds a plant or animal

extinction   the process by which a plant or animal species ceases to exist

fossil   the remains of an ancient plant or animal

gorge   a deep, narrow canyon with steep, rocky walls

habitat	the physical surroundings where a living thing makes its home
hominid	the earliest ancestor of human beings
jungle	tropical land covered with a dense growth of trees, vines, and bushes
kangas	brightly colored cloth squares that wrap into a native African costume
omnivorous	eating both animals and plants
"pant-hoot"	a loud call made by chimpanzees
predator	an animal that hunts other animals for food
rain forest	a densely forested region found in areas of heavy rainfall near the equator
savannah	a broad, flat tropical grassland
species	a group of similar plants or animals that can produce offspring
tool	a device used to do work
vegetarian	a person or animal that does not eat meat
wildlife	animals or plants living in a natural state
wildlife observer	a person who watches and records the behavior of animals in their natural habitat
wildlife sanctuary	an area of land or water set aside as a protected home for wildlife

Index